piano
vocal
guitar

the *Best* of
stacey
kent

Cover photo by Kim Knott

ISBN 0-634-07884-4

HAL•LEONARD®
CORPORATION
7777 W. BLUEMOUND RD. P.O. BOX 13819 MILWAUKEE, WI 53213

Visit Hal Leonard Online at
www.halleonard.com

contents

THE BEST IS YET TO COME

Words by CAROLYN LEIGH
Music by CY COLEMAN

Moderately, with a beat

Out of the tree of life___ I just picked me a plum,___

You came a-long and ev - 'ry-thing's start-in' to hum;___

Still it's a real good bet___ The Best Is Yet To Come,

THE BOY NEXT DOOR

Words and Music by HUGH MARTIN
and RALPH BLANE

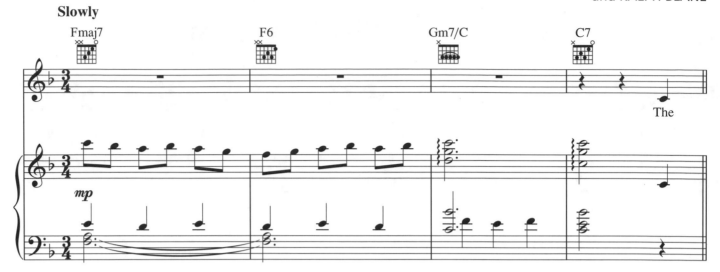

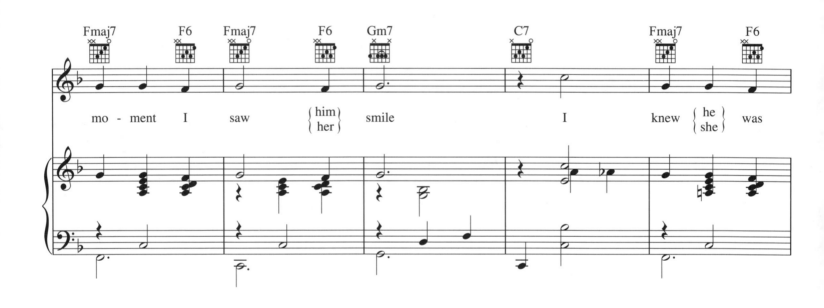

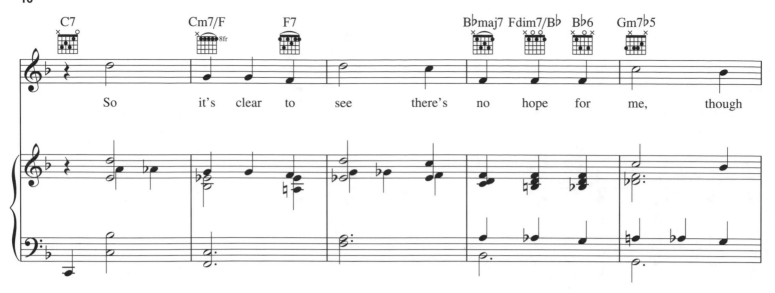

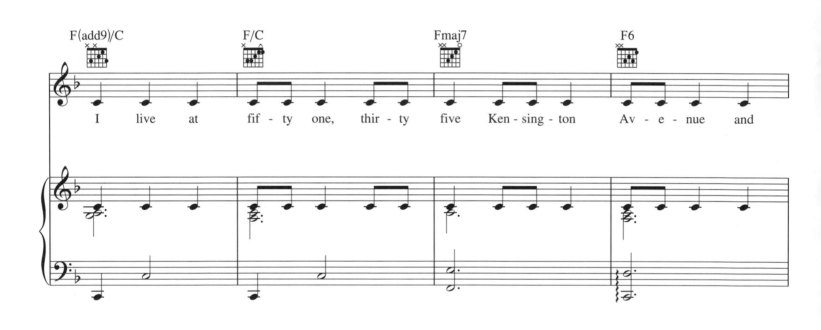

door af - fec - tion for me won't dis - play._____ I

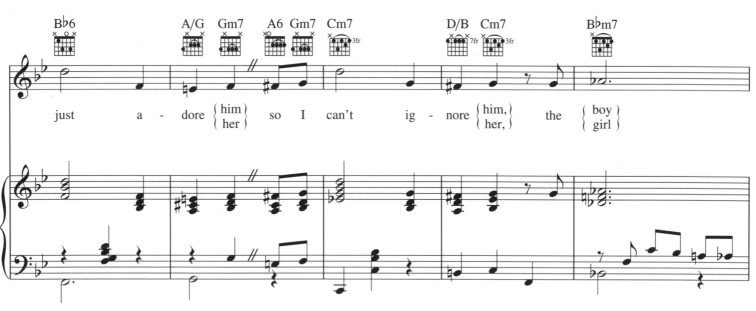

just a - dore {him}{her} so I can't ig - nore {him,}{her,} the {boy}{girl}

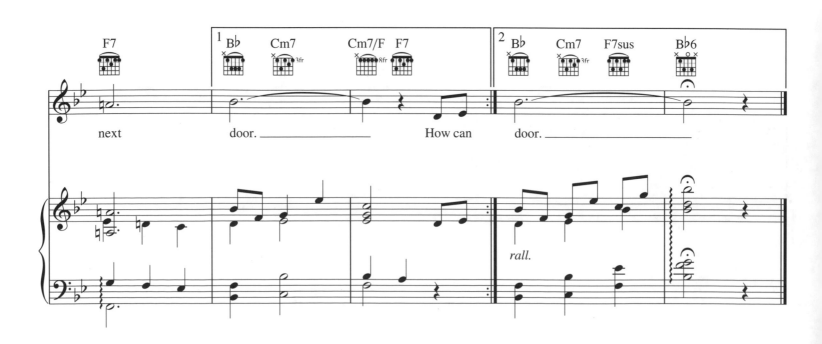

next door._____ How can door._____

DREAMSVILLE

Lyrics by JAY LIVINGSTON and RAY EVANS
Music by HENRY MANCINI

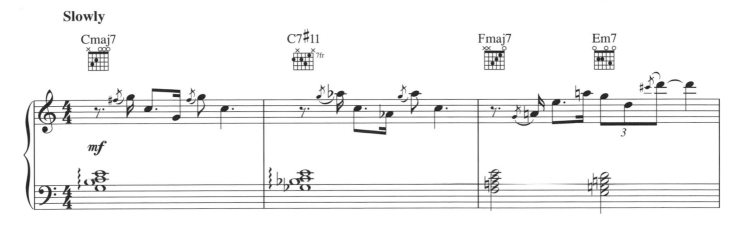

I'm in Dreams-ville __ hold - ing

you; a dream - y view, just we

HE LOVES AND SHE LOVES

from FUNNY FACE

Music and Lyrics by GEORGE GERSHWIN
and IRA GERSHWIN

I GUESS I'LL HAVE TO CHANGE
MY PLAN

Words by HOWARD DIETZ
Music by ARTHUR SCHWARTZ

I WON'T DANCE

from ROBERTA

Words and Music by JIMMY McHUGH, DOROTHY FIELDS,
JEROME KERN, OSCAR HAMMERSTEIN II and OTTO HARBACH

I'M PUTTING ALL MY EGGS IN ONE BASKET

from the Motion Picture FOLLOW THE FLEET

Words and Music by
IRVING BERLIN

I'VE GOT A CRUSH ON YOU

Music and Lyrics by GEORGE GERSHWIN
and IRA GERSHWIN

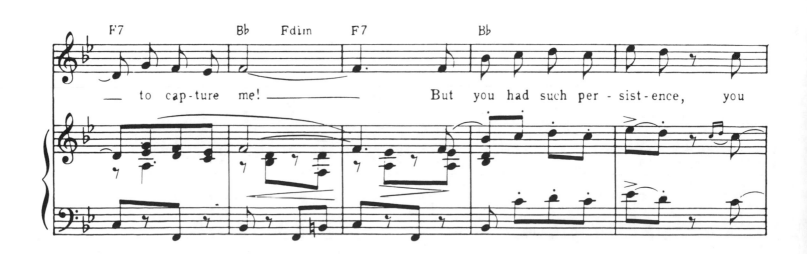

IT NEVER ENTERED MY MIND

from HIGHER AND HIGHER

Words by LORENZ HART
Music by RICHARD RODGERS

PEOPLE WILL SAY WE'RE IN LOVE

from OKLAHOMA!

Lyrics by OSCAR HAMMERSTEIN II
Music by RICHARD RODGERS

SAY IT ISN'T SO

Words and Music by
IRVING BERLIN

SHALL WE DANCE?

from THE KING AND I

Lyrics by OSCAR HAMMERSTEIN II
Music by RICHARD RODGERS

Brightly (moderato)

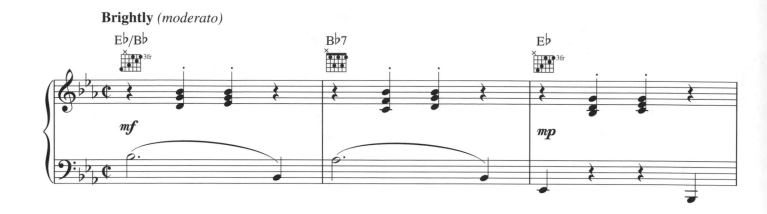

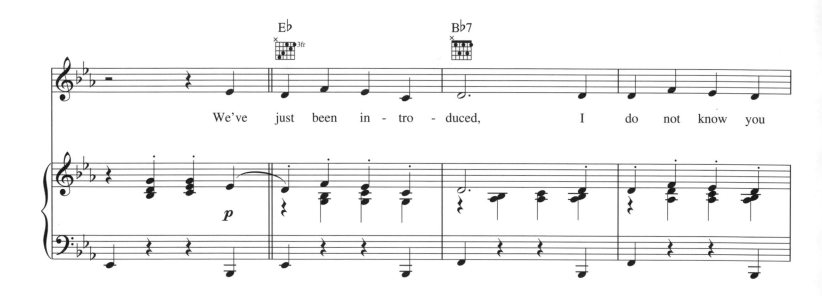

We've just been in-tro-duced, I do not know you well. But when the mu-sic start-ed, some-thing drew me to your side. So

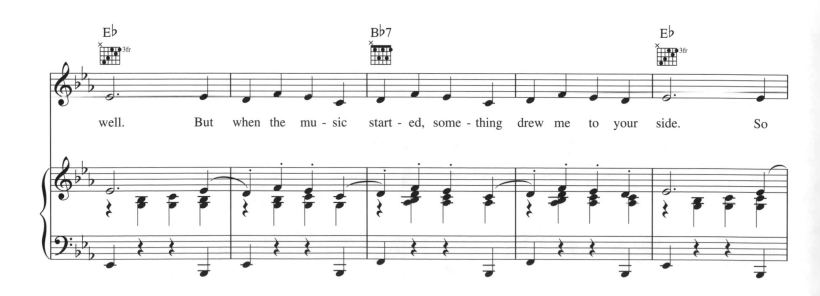

(Love Is)
THE TENDER TRAP

Words by SAMMY CAHN
Music by JAMES VAN HEUSEN

THANKS FOR THE MEMORY

from the Paramount Picture BIG BROADCAST OF 1938

Words and Music by LEO ROBIN
and RALPH RAINGER

Thanks for the mem-o-ry of
Thanks for the mem-o-ry of

can-dle-light and wine, ___ cas-tles on the Rhine, ___ the
sen-ti-men-tal verse, ___ noth-ing in my purse, ___ and

Par-the-non and mo-ments on the Hud-son Riv-er Line. ___ How
chuck-les when the preach-er said, "For bet-ter or for worse." ___ How

THEY CAN'T TAKE THAT AWAY FROM ME

from THE BARKLEYS OF BROADWAY

Music and Lyrics by GEORGE GERSHWIN
and IRA GERSHWIN

With movement

Our ro - mance won't end on a sor - row - ful note,

Though by to - mor - row you're gone; The song is end - ed,

but as the song - writ - er wrote, The mel - o - dy ling - ers

TOO DARN HOT

from KISS ME, KATE

Words and Music by
COLE PORTER

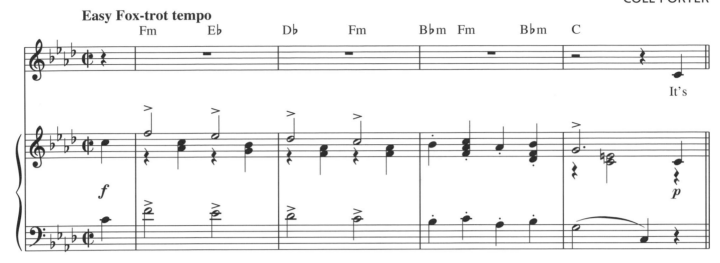

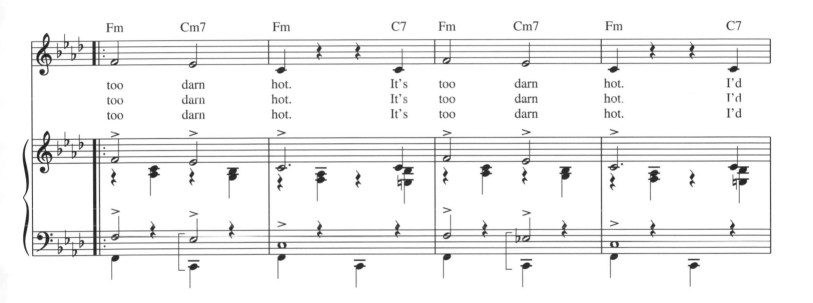

THEY SAY IT'S WONDERFUL

from the Stage Production ANNIE GET YOUR GUN

Words and Music by
IRVING BERLIN

THE TROLLEY SONG

from MEET ME IN ST. LOUIS

Music by RALPH BLANE
Lyric by HUGH MARTIN

Bb   F9/Bb   Bbmaj7   F9/Bb

start - ed to yen, so I count - ed to ten, then I
start - ed to yen, so I count - ed to ten, then I

Bb   F9sus F7 Bb7sus   Bb7

count - ed to ten a - gain.
count - ed to ten a - gain.

gliss. on white keys

Eb6

Eb6

"Clang, clang, clang," went the trol - ley,
"Clang, clang, clang," went the trol - ley,

WHEN YOUR LOVER HAS GONE

Words and Music by
E.A. SWAN

VIOLETS FOR YOUR FURS

By TOM ADAIR and MATT DENNIS